# So Lucky You're My DAD

LET ME TELL YOU WHY

DAD—DO YOU KNOW WHAT I JUST REALIZED?

MY LIFE IS PRETTY GREAT.

AND DO YOU KNOW WHO HAD SOMETHING TO DO WITH THAT?

YOU!

LET ME TELL YOU WHY.

THIS BOOK IS A CELEBRATION OF *you*—
A GREAT *Big* CHEER
FOR ALL YOU'VE DONE FOR ME
AND A PARTY FOR ALL WE'VE SHARED.

I'VE FILLED IT WITH MY FAVORITE THINGS ABOUT YOU,

THE VERY BEST MEMORIES I HAVE OF YOU,

PLUS ALL THE THINGS YOU DO THAT AMAZE ME, IMPRESS ME, AND MAKE ME FEEL CAPABLE OF ANYTHING—BECAUSE...

______________________________________

______________________________________.

MY WHOLE LIFE, I'VE HAD A FRONT ROW SEAT TO YOUR

MAGIC.

When I was a kid,
I THOUGHT
I WAS SO lucky to
have a DAD AS...

- ☐ CARING
- ☐ HILARIOUS
- ☐ STRONG
- ☐ SMART
- ☐ HIP
- ☐ SUPPORTIVE
- ☐ WISE
- ☐ ADVENTUROUS
- ☐ KNOWLEDGEABLE
- ☐ CREATIVE
- ☐ LOVING
- ☐ THOUGHTFUL
- ☐ PLAYFUL

...as you.

YOU WERE THE ONLY DAD
I KNEW WHO

______________________________,

AND I BRAGGED TO ALL MY
FRIENDS ABOUT YOUR

______________________________.

# PLUS, I ALWAYS HAD THE...

(circle one on each side)

| | |
|---|---|
| BEST | outfits |
| MOST FUN | meals |
| COOLEST | stories |
| WILDEST | advice |
| SWEETEST | birthday parties |
| MOST MAGICAL | vacations |
| MOST LEGENDARY | role model |
| FUNNIEST | adventures |

...THANKS TO you.

GROWING UP, I LOVED THAT I GOT TO SEE YOUR

______________________________

SIDE.

LIKE THAT ONE TIME you

______________________________

______________________________.

N
W
E
S

How is it
THAT OUT OF
ALL
THE DADS in THE
WORLD,
you ENDED up
MINE?

WHEN I WAS YOUNGER,
I THOUGHT you MADE

____________________

LOOK SO EASY.

AS I GOT OLDER,
I REALIZED HOW INCREDIBLY

____________________

you REALLY WERE.

REMEMBER MY

PHASE? Yikes.

IS NOW A GOOD TIME TO SAY SORRY FOR

?

(Really.)

## ON THE HARD DAYS, you COULD'VE...

- [ ] PACKED ME UP IN A BOX AND SHIPPED ME HALFWAY AROUND THE WORLD
- [ ] SAID NO TO EVERYTHING FOR THE REST OF TIME
- [ ] GIVEN UP AND SET ME FREE IN THE FOREST
- [ ] TAKEN THE NEXT FLIGHT TO SPAIN AND NEVER COME BACK

... BUT *you* DIDN'T.
(THANKS!)

INSTEAD, *you*

_______________________________.

I KNOW, I KNOW,

YOU'RE MY DAD—

IT'S YOUR JOB.

BUT I'VE NEVER FELT MORE LOVED AND SUPPORTED THAN WHEN YOU

______________________________.

...AND YOU STILL MAKE ME FEEL 100 FEET TALL, EVERY TIME YOU

______________________________.

YOU AND ME?
WE'RE LIKE MUSHROOMS—
SNEAKILY CONNECTED
JUST BENEATH THE SURFACE.

I MEAN, I GET SOME OF MY BEST QUALITIES FROM YOU:

... AND PROBABLY SOME OF MY WEIRDEST, SUCH AS

________________________________.

I LOVE CALLING YOU WHENEVER SOMETHING BIG HAPPENS, LIKE ______________________.

BUT YOU'RE THERE FOR THE EVERYDAY STUFF TOO, LIKE...

1. ______________________

2. ______________________

3. ______________________

HERE'S THE THING—YOU MAY THINK I'M GROWN UP, BUT I STILL NEED YOUR...

- ☐ REGULAR CHATS
- ☐ LEVEL-HEADED ADVICE
- ☐ WARM HUGS
- ☐ FIVE-STAR COOKING
- ☐ LITTLE PEP TALKS
- ☐ BIG IDEAS
- ☐ ____________________

...TO GET ME THROUGH.

AND THERE'S NO ONE ELSE I'D

RATHER ______________________________

WITH THAN YOU.

(TRUly!)

THE WILD THING IS, YOU'RE NOT *JUST* MY DAD.

YOU HAVE A WHOLE INSPIRING LIFE DRIZZLED ON TOP.

WHEN I WAS A KID, I WAS FASCINATED BY ALL THE THINGS YOU MADE TIME FOR (JUST FOR YOU), LIKE...

1.

2.

3.

...AND I watched YOU WORK hard TO

________________________________.

REMEMBER WHEN YOU WANTED TO TRY SOMETHING NEW AND ______________________?

I THOUGHT THAT WAS SO COOL.

LOOKING BACK, IT'S CLEAR YOUR PASSION FOR

______________________

RUBBED OFF ON ME.

IF I HAD TO LIST YOUR BIGGEST ACHIEVEMENTS, THEY WOULD BE:

1. ME (OF COURSE)
2.
3.
4.
SEE WHAT I MEAN?
IMPRESSIVE STUFF.

11 : 26
1
3
4
5
8
9
10
11
12
13
14

BUT WHAT I LOVE MOST IS THAT *you* STILL FIND ROOM IN *your* SCHEDULE (AND HEART) FOR ME.

WITH ALL THE TIME YOU SPEND

________________________________,

AND ALL THE FUN YOU NOW HAVE

________________________________.

...BECAUSE WE'VE GOT PLACES
LEFT TO GO,
PUZZLES TO PIECE TOGETHER,
AND TREASURES STILL TO UNCOVER.

IF I STRUCK IT RICH,
I'D TAKE YOU

______________________________.

We'd BRING

______________________________

AND PASS THE days

______________________________.

But I DON'T NEED A CENT
TO HAVE A GOOD TIME WITH YOU—

just ______________________________

AND ______________________________.

13 05
11 : 26

IF I COULD REWIND THE CLOCK, I'D WANT TO RELIVE THE DAY WE

______________________________

______________________________

______________________________.

AS WE BOTH GET OLDER...

I HOPE WE CAN

_______________________________________

_______________________________________.

...AND I HOPE

WE NEVER STOP

_______________________________________

_______________________________________.

DAD — YOU MAKE ME FEEL LUCKY. LUCKY TO HAVE ENDED UP EXACTLY WHERE I NEED TO BE:

- ☐ MAKING MOVES AND DOING RAD THINGS
- ☐ CONTRIBUTING TO THE WORLD IN MY OWN WAY
- ☐ DREAMING BIG ABOUT WHAT'S NEXT
- ☐ COZY IN THIS LIFE I'M BUILDING
- ☐ SECURE AND LOVED NO MATTER WHAT

I DON'T SAY IT ENOUGH,
BUT IT'S TRUE:

______________________________

______________________________.

THE TRUTH IS...
WITHOUT YOU,
I WOULDN'T BE ME.

THANKS FOR (PRETTY MUCH)
EVERYTHING.

WITH LOVE, ______________________
(A VERY LUCKY PERSON)

COMPENDIUM®
live inspired

Written by: Danielle Leduc McQueen
Illustrated by: Kerrie McNeill
Edited by: Bailey Vega
Art Directed by: Megan Gandt

ISBN: 978-1-957891-37-8



This book may be ordered directly from the publisher, but please try your local bookstore first. Call us at 800.91.IDEAS, or come see our full line of inspiring products at live-inspired.com.

1st printing. Printed in China with soy inks on FSC®-Mix certified paper.

*Create meaningful moments with gifts that inspire.*

CONNECT WITH US

live-inspired.com | sayhello@compendiuminc.com

@compendiumliveinspired
#compendiumliveinspired